AF454092

Feeling My Existence

Shawn Akrawi

CONTENTS

Dedication

This book is dedicated to my lovely wife, Camilla, whom I love so dearly. I also dedicate this book to my dear father Husam Akrawi for teaching me to love poetry and to love humanity.

Introduction

I know that I exist because I feel my existence. I am all the feelings that emerge when I sense the reflection of the universe that I am a part of. I am a creator and a creation beginning from nothing to flow along a river of knowledge rushing toward an unforeseeable end. Until then, I will experience many things, and the experiences will make me feel.

Without my feelings I would probably not have learned about life and about my existence. My feelings are the differentiators that form my unique self above existence and empowers me to turn torment to joy or fear to love. I am one with the logics of everything until I stop to feel.

Feelings, the knowledge that remains a secret for me about myself, inside myself, among so many things, beings and thoughts. My feelings create me as they spread my parts in an unknown existence and make me long to learn about existing.

My feelings existed before I knew that I existed and the same feelings evolved to teach me about myself and about my existence. Like a school of life inside me growing and building my understanding of myself. Who can teach me more than my needs, fears, my hunger, and the feeling of satisfaction? So my inner feelings build my truth, and my truth is the world of my existence.

With every breath, I learn by being molded in the complexity of life that turns fragments of senses to thoughts that turns to feelings creating the consciousness inside my mind.

A consciousness originating from the body of life, carrying the code of the universe through what seems to be an eternity. The code that created me and made me inhale the first breath and open my eyes to see and hear the waves of life. The code that taught me to learn and think so I may understand my surroundings and bring the past and the unborn future to my present inside the world of my feelings.

My feelings make me search, love, long, struggle to survive, and understand my experiences. I feel when I speak, listen, and distinguish wisdom from foolishness and truth from lies. I feel when I read and write poetry, where I gather my thoughts and summarize my mentality. It is an attempt to recreate my feelings with words, not necessarily the truth, but rather my perception of truth and how I react to it.

What I write is my passion reflecting existence where I visualize my world to understand myself in my thoughts. I am in the words of my poems, in the essence of my thoughts and the shapes of my imagination. I can strive to be what I can imagine and nothing beyond, but I can be less than what's possible if I don't see the opportunities that seem to be unreal and sometimes unnatural. I am my ultimate judge, and only I can be me. I know who and what I am, as I constantly live inside my thoughts and inside the environments I exist in.

I don't know myself outside myself or outside my own thoughts. Yet, inside myself I can be anything I wish inside the boundaries of my feelings and the captivity of my beliefs. In my imagination, I can travel in space time as I please, without traveling, and live outside my life without living.

I still don't know what the meaning of my life is, or if there is a meaning at all. My ignorance may be the meaning of my life, as it is the driving force for me to seek wisdom as I experience life.

It is mysterious how the searching and the finding grow and disappear as one and at the same time. My life is one trace of that mystery created by the feelings of my existence.

Now, I invite you to my world and into my inner thoughts in these stories. The tales of my world where I can learn the knowledge of several millennials while trying to feel and survive the last moment. My world where I reflect several universes through my senses and turn everything to impressions that I understand by feeling my existence.

Among the most important chapters of my life are the feelings of love, the feelings of faith, and the feelings of existence. These are the basis and the chapters of this book that I want to share with you. After reading the poems, I hope that you can experience, feel, and create new thoughts in your own world to enrich your existence and stimulate what makes you human.

So please read about my feelings and thoughts given new life in the world of words.

Chapter 1 – Of Love

In my world of love there are oceans of joy and sorrow
The sky is made of satisfaction and discontentment
And life springs from feelings of lust, fear, and comfort

Beauty

Beauty, speak no beautiful words
You are the inspiration of beautiful words
My words, in a mystical phrase
In a poem of your magical ways
Words melting with magnificence
As my eyes meet your elegance
Your truth and my imagination
Rhyming with my passion
A poem...a tale
From my mind
Written in my heart
Rhyming with you
Teach me your beauty
And I will teach you of beautiful words
Teach me of nothing
And of nothing
I will learn of everything
Be the substance of my life
Stay with me
While I dedicate to you my world
And whisper my love for you as I breathe

Just be
Let me speak of beauty
Let me speak of you
Of your eyes
Your touch
Your everything
Let me shape my words
As you are shaping my feelings

Just be
And purify my thoughts
With your gentle smile
Slay my roots
Destroy me

Then raise me
To immortality
Let me grow in your heaven
Cut the veins of my knowledge
And question my truth
Erase my age and grant me youth
Just be beauty
Just be you

How

How did you manage to penetrate my soul
Find its hidden heart
Easily break its shell
And melt with its core

How did you manage to fit my paradise
Into your beauty
Stop the course of time
And be the only one to adore

How did you manage to hold my hand
Fill my body with life
Then fill life with love
And fill love with your magnificence

How did you manage what others have failed
Erase my pain
Stop my fears
And fill my guilt with innocence

Everything and nothing

There is a kiss concealed in your lips
There is a secret adding beauty to your eyes
There is confidence in your smile
And a distance wishing to die

There is softness in your voice
Soft
As if it's telling the hardships of your life
And of the captivity of your love
Softly
Singing the freedom song of your soul

Mysterious
As you reflect beauty itself
Miraculous
In your simple truth
Marvelous
Forcing me to long...too long

I can be your pillow
I can be your dreams
I can be an arrow
Traveling through your winds
Touching your heart
Melting in your fantasies
I can be your everything
I can be your nothing

Your spirit is calling me
Unheard, unseen, and untouched
Yet felt
With all my senses
In a vision beyond my visions
Convincing me
You can be my everything
You can be my nothing

Your prison

Your eyes imprison my soul
To keep the secrets of my confessions
And bury my sinful truth

In your prison
I am free beyond freedom
In your silence
I hear more words than life can contain
In your blue eyes
My sense sleeps
Never to wake again

From the past

Do you remember the boy
Do you remember the joy
Remember the childish purity of his heart
His wild uncontrollable love
The madness of his wishes and dreams
Do you remember me?

Captured by your beauty
To be a prisoner of your cruelty
And tortured by the ways of passion
To deny myself
To deny you
Do you deny me?

In the days of yesterday
Singing forgotten tunes
To an unbeaten rhythm
And adding tales to my unwritten diary
Do you remember the melody?

Twelve turns to one

Twelve turns to one
Two along one world
Revolving its sun
A thousand times
Blessed by your love
Magically doing the undone

Now, one is my world
And you are my sun

The same road

You are the same road that I walked
With her
Do you remember?
How could even your stones forget?
The touch of her feet
The rhythm of her steps

As in my future
She is missing
As in my heart
She is always there
Mourn with me, oh road of my love

The tree on the sidewalk
Still beautiful
Yet its beauty revealing sadness
The nest of the birds
Still wonderful
Yet empty
Like the heart of my love

Do you feel my lonely steps?
My abandoned soul
Missing her laughter and joy
Her magnificence and her softness
Wish with me, oh road
The return of my love

As every step left a mark on your face
Every moment with her left a mark in my spirit
Where no other is to go
Nothing to be planted
Nothing to grow
Remember with me, oh road
The grace of my love

You are the same road that I walked
With her
Do you remember?

In your eyes

In your eyes
I see the images of my life
In your eyes
I see the fruits of my sacrifice
Lust and anger
Pleasure and pain
My whole world is in your eyes
In your eyes
I am the prisoner of love
With broken wings
Trying to fly to your heaven
I see the depth of the skies
I see the truth and the lies
I see paradise burning to ashes
And hell frozen to ice
In your eyes
I see my visions more clearly
I see my sun rise
Where certainty is a surprise
All of me and my feelings
I see
In your eyes

Between

Between your glance and your voice
My confusion is born
Between your breasts and your waist
My passion wishes me to be
Between your lips
I wish to obtain my breath
Between your eyes
My visions I wish to see

Between your left and your right
Not above or below
Only between

My angel

My angel is not of heaven
Heaven is of my angel
The dawn of gentleness comes through her blue
More blue than blue
Her eyes, her blue
As she wakes to bless the world
And makes her wonders visible

My angel is not a dream
Dreams are of my angel
With wings made of passion
She sails across my sky
Her smile calls me to paradise
Where she teaches me how to fly
To the extreme of all my senses

My angel is not of my world
My world is of my angel
Beauty sets and rests with her
In the shade of her consciousness
In the tales of her eyes
Beauty wakes and sleeps with her
As I stand in the shadows of my angel

Seasons

As the seasons are made of motion
Life itself is made of seasons
What else is there to choose if one wishes life
than traveling with time without reasons?

My seasons are only two
One is happy and one is sad
One is short and one is stretched

The air I breathe has two odors
One of fire and one of flowers
One rare and one frequent

So, I drink my wine
Until my world completes a thousand circles
While dreaming of a different reality

For what other way is there to taste the fruits of life
If the fruits of my liking are forbidden
Unless I intoxicate and confuse my sanity

I choose life
Unable to choose the seasons
I travel with time without reasons

Secret Love

I love you
Like an orphan loves his parents
Like the silent bird loves his song
Like a dreamer lost in his happy dream
At the end of an endless stream

I love you
Beyond sense
In a secret
In solitude
Silently from distance
More than longing
More than sadness

I love you
Beyond pain
In anger
In shame
In tormenting existence
More than reason
More than madness

Imprisoned in my truth
Silently from distance
I love you

The Painter

Who is the painter?
Who paints beauty with the color of deception
And motives of happiness with strokes of lies
Who is the painter?
That draws boxes in circles
Curves in straight lines
To illustrate my dreams
Who is the painter?
Who shares the meaning of life with me
Yet makes the red of my roses pale
Who is the painter?
That silences my heart
With symbols of his truth
And makes my tears invisible
Who is the painter?
That embodies my greatest thoughts in a single woman
And deteriorates my mind in the shape of her shadow
Who is the painter?
Who unveils the secrets of my soul with pigments of shame?
Keeping my secrets in a dream within the dream within dreams
Who is the painter?
Imprisoning me in the Holy Spirit as a sinner
And in sinful acts as a saint
Who is the painter?
Why is he painting?

The Glass of Wine

Aren't you the blood of grapes?
Aren't you the blood of a god?
Either way, you are to be present in my blood

Help me unlearn what I have learned
By sacrificing my nature
Dragging my pride in the mud

Are you the reason for my tears?
Clear, unlike the uncertain mind they obey
Are you the lionheart of my fear?
Through the unrest of my night and my painful day

Make me see why I am loved and rejected
Unveil to me the secrets behind the lies
Or poison my knowledge and kill my will
And silence the part that cries

Put my sorrow to sleep
For my soul needs to sleep
And my mind needs to rest

Fill me with illusions
Fill my shame with sympathy
Change my worst with your best

Fill me
Poison me
Heal me
Blessed glass of wine

Stay

Read my tears in this verse
Feel my passion within phrases
Close your eyes to dream with me
And stay...stay
Along with your beauty that fills my soul
Among all thoughts
That energizes my will
To long and to Love
Stay, in the bosom of wonders
You as the wonder of my mind
Beyond the fences of the days
Outside the gates of the nights
Stay with me
Stay and wish for time to die
And forever to be born
Where I worship your eyes
And your body that forms my shrine
Where I pray
For you to stay

Stay with my ways
In a place where one dream is life
One reality is not
Fear shapes laughter
Where comfort lives in lies
And the spirit is blue as your eyes
Tears crushing my strength
And a shadow is the only evidence of light
Where life is thrown away
Unless you stay

She reads my poem

She reads my poem
Turning rust to gold
Gazing at the words until they awake
Saying them as they wish to be told

She reads my poem
And simple feelings turn to passion
Giving life to the lifeless
With a voice of affection

She reads my pain between the lines
And attends my wounds
With loving eyes
Making my soul breathe her Love

Blessed is the name of Love
When embraced by her lips
Reborn waves to sound in the mist
Of a soul lost in the shade of her eclipse
She reads my poem
Turning my longing to a prayer
Filling the temple of my heart
With faith and despair

She reads my poem
My mind, my faith, my inner
On a thin paper
Of a hope...sadly thinner

More

I write my verse with words
You write yours with splendor
In rhymes I only reflect your colors
You are the master of my feelings
The beautiful and tender

You are more than my art
More than the spirit of my fantasies
More than my thoughts
More than my freedom and liberty

It's hard to tell of my passion
It's more than words can tell
More than laughter tells of happiness
Or silent tears wishing to yell

It's hard to gently speak of pain
Or painfully speak of you
Or truthfully tell a lie
Or lie of what is true

Lost on the single road of my mind
Seeking what's yet to be found
Looking for your shadow
Listening for a sound

Full of infatuation and lust
Looking for more
Of your magnificence
And every time I find your truth

I find you more
More than any description
More than any poem
Simply more

In you

Don't describe me
Hide your thoughts
Hide me near to your dreams
Near to your truth
Free of manipulation

In you
With your thoughts
In secrecy
Untouched by my own will
Unharmed by my mentality

A part of purity
A part of you
I'm in you
Don't describe me
Hide me

Embrace me

Embrace me
Then let us close our eyes
To blind our senses
And reshape our selves
From within the uncertain

Embrace me
And let us hear nothing
But the longing of our souls
For the stories of the past
Forgotten since an unknown when

Embrace me
And kill my freedom
Then leave me in captivity
In the prison of sentiments
And maybe visit me now and then

Embrace me
Beyond the physical world
For I long for your embrace
As I stand outside life
Longing to live again

Wed

Unmistakable
Undoubtable
I saw the truth
Embraced by Love
In the most beautiful of places
Where the clear sky and the sea
Witnessed your eyes
And learn to be blue
In a cave of faith
Sheltered by bare trees
In the bosom of a holy mountain
Where words of wisdom
Melted with the magic of love
Shaking the core of life
Exploding in emotions
To rest in the comfort of confidence
In the temple of tomorrow
Two voices formed a prayer
As spirits became spiritual
And dreams became senses

Calmer than calm
Beyond imagination
I understood
Why I love you
While your beauty took me to
Where my body became my spirit
Where my end
Gave birth to us

Hide me in your hidden world

Hide me in your hidden world
Along with what lives in you
Where feelings turn to memories
And beauty sleeps with infamy

Hide me in your hidden world
Alone...with your solitude
Where I can be loved
And embraced in secrecy

Hide me in your hidden world
Where fate is unknown
Then tell me where I lost myself
Tell me where I lost my days

Hide me in your hidden self
To melt in your heart
Then shine your light on me
Lighten my spirit and darken my ways
Hide me in your life
And save me from time
In the smallest of your places
Safe beyond all my doubts

Hide me in your hidden world
Bury me in your earth
And feed me from within
Then forget my whereabouts

Captured

Captured in small drops
Is my fear and sorrow
Washing you from my pain

Yet every drop fails its mission
As the heart of my memory
Paints your face again

Captured in your beautiful eyes
Is Love and a hope
On the way to go insane

And thoughts are no longer thoughts
They are passionate feelings
As the heart replaces the brain

Captured in a dream with you
In the purest of sins
Losing when I gain

Timeless without time and room
Is the eternal Love
In life it grows, till death to remain

Blessed flower

You were born with beauty that nature gave
Free without a master or a slave
Painted by your inner self and forced to behave
In a certain fashion from birth to the grave

You are to live in the wonder of existence
Share your time in a measured distance
To end your form to form another
Before that, speak to me like sister to brother

Tell me, as you are yellow
And I pale
Tell me flower of my Love
With only truth in your tale

From her hands I received you
After she blessed you with her kiss
Challenge my imagination
Tell me of the taste of her lips

Tell me the secrets she whispered
Tell me of her warm breath
Of the passion in her soul
Tell me of life after death

Chapter 2 – Of Beliefs

In the world of my beliefs there are mountains of infinity
The fields are made of light and darkness
And what grows there is consciousness and tranquility

The Mystery of Existence

Would you rather be homeless
In a world of unhappy homes?
Would you still pray
In temples lacking domes?
Will you give up your joy
If it met losing your pains?
Will you give up your losses
If it met losing your gains?
Do you embrace your fears
To show your bravery?
Do you deny your defeats
When you dream of victory?

Would you rather be silent
If no one hears your voice?
Would you still choose
Without understanding your choice?
Oh, you who seek the secret of life
What if there is no secret?
Oh, you who seek the mystery of existence
What if there is no mystery?

What if there is nothing more
Than a fragment of existence
In an eternal universe
Turning to feelings
To build your essence

Would you still move
If everything around you stood still?
Would you choose eternity
If it meant losing your will?
Oh, you who seek divine salvation
Have you found your earthly captivity?
Oh, you who blindly seek your freedom
What if your freedom turns to slavery?

In the riddle of existence
Behind unknown secrets
What do you expect to find
In your uncertain limited time
And your unlimited mind?

You who seek the mysteries of existence
What if there are no mysteries?

Faith

Faith is when everything
Settled and unsettled
In your thoughts seeks a meaning
Hope, belief, doubt
In a cold or a burning core
Adding honor or demeaning

When everything you wish is impossible
You bow down to see the invisible
And repeat your selfish verse
Wishing for nothing but your way
And when asked, you lie answering
It's only for the good you pray

Seeking for the creation in the creator
While you seek for the creator in the creation
Seeking for salvation in your addiction
Seeking for honor in the deception
Finding your forgiveness in your redemption

What is your faith?
Do you believe in your thoughts
In your understanding of things
Is your faith beyond your deeds
Is your faith short of your needs

Can the blind believe in the light
Can the deaf hear the story of divinity
Can the living live to die
And die believing in eternity

Do you believe what you see
Do you believe what you hear
Do you believe in what you love
Or do you believe what you fear

Is your faith the life you have
The life you lack
Or how you wish to live
Is your faith one
Is your faith two
Is your faith a story or more
Is your faith a truth or true

Are you lost
Do you seek yourself or another
From the past
Or in your future
And who do you find
In your roots
Your branches or your leaves
For mankind seek themselves in a faith
But lose themselves in their beliefs

The Word

Who brought the word
To the world
And planted his way
In the heart of humanity
To live beyond humans
Through humans
Love through life
Life through love

Who brought the world
Through a word
And gave man
Truth and lies
Of the minds
To describe anything
In everything
And unmatter the matter

The world is a word
as the word is the world
Of a beginning
Now forgotten
Of an end
Still unheard

When I look toward the sky

I look toward the sky
To find myself
Or to find you in my inner
I feel you when I seek comfort
I cry for you when I'm fearful
I cry for you when I'm in pain
I look for you to understand
What is beyond my understanding
Who are you
If not my self in another being
My self without a shape
Can you see your self
In the shape of a man
And find yourself
In the mist of his thoughts?
I can see you shaping me
I can hear me calling you
To call me
To guide me
To where I wish not to go
Can you see my visions
Or are you all of my visions?
Can you hear my song
Or are you my songs?
Be in my thoughts
Oh, you who I love and not fear

Be near
For you distance
Is my journey to nowhere
A strive for nothing
I wish to know you
More than myself
I wish to be you
More than myself
And so, I look toward the sky

To begin
I look toward the sky
For an end

34

My God

They taught me to believe in a creator
They taught me to prepare for a judgment
They planted in me a feeling
A faith, a doubt, a hope, and a torment
And they called it God

They spoke of almightiness
That gives existence a beginning
And deprives the beginning of an end
In a game without losing or winning
And they called it eternity

They told me God is my choice
My inexplicable wish to dream
My shelter where I am unhidden
Where I can fail and redeem
And they called it serenity

They told me God is the fountain of joy
The heart of compassion
A light shining through
Forgiveness and reconciliation
And they called that Christianity

They told me God is unborn
An experience beyond my experience
Creating me free in his image
To kneel and show obedience
They called it divinity

Then I learned that God is my thoughts
Of myself outside myself
Longing to get inside
To complete the self
And I call it Me

Then I wonder who I was
And why was I a creation
With a God of imagination
Beyond imagination
And I call it life

Then I closed my eyes
And open the heart of my thoughts
I saw colors beyond my sight
I felt free tied in knots
And I call it wisdom

Then I heard a voice
From me to me to be braver
A whisper echoing louder than all sounds
Repeating the song of life forever
And that is the voice of my God

So then God is eternity
In my limited life
And the serenity
In my precarious existence
Or unreal tranquility
In a judgmental truth
God may be the divinity
That I need to see
To learn about me
And to feel free
When I imagine life
And strive to be one
With an invisible wisdom
And be the created creator
Appearing to disappear
To serve the greater

Doubting what I believe
Believing my doubts
Floating in floods of uncertainty
Drowning in my droughts

Seeking in the stories I learned
And kneeling before nothingness
Kneeling before myself
In my consciousness
To hear my whispering voice
And learn of what I know
And embrace my choice
Forming my mentality
To survive reality
And bow before existence
To learn to feel
The shape of my God

I believe the unbelievable

I believe the unbelievable
Inside the core I call my soul
Sensing nothing more or less than life
Walking toward an unavoidable goal

I believe the unbelievable
Inside me that I call my call
Leading me from nowhere to nowhere
Teaching me to crawl...stand and fall

Learning to dream of dreams
To believe and feel the possible
Entering an unreal reality of things
Stubbornly defying the impossible

To dream beyond life of the unknown
Before birth of the unborn motherless
Of a beginning before the beginning
Of the unbelievably endless

In a world of confusion I seek certainty
And in my certainty I am confused
I live in the images of my memories
Of what I used and misused

I believe in the silent voice guiding me
To a path beyond words
Telling me to laugh...to cry...to speak...to live
And build a world unlike all worlds

Unable to stop, unwilling to forget
Too proud to deny my shameless confessions
Of the unbelievable inside my thoughts
And the ways of my conceptions

Nobody can see the world of my solitude

As my entire world is an invisible sight
A deep ocean of emotions
With waves of despair and delight

I believe in the unbelievable lies
To numb the truth of my reality
I believe in what is beyond belief
Beyond infinity and divinity

I am the subject of my consciousness
The judge and the criminal
In my temple of life
I am the ethics and the unethical

I believe in a vision that only one can see
I believe through one life...one reality
I believe in the unbelievable
I believe the only one that lives in me

My faith

I believe
I need my faith
Where the truth lies
Beyond the light and darkness
Of my days

Where I'm more than life
By understanding my limits
And infinite in my thoughts
Calling divinity
With a magical phrase

Endless before the beginning
A creation within a creation
A winner without winning
In a reality of imagination

My faith makes me deny myself
To be myself
Outside myself
Living from within
Battling my needs
Cursing my curses
Repeating my creeds
My faith spreads my thoughts
Between strength and weakness
Rushing along a stream of ethics
To see my sins and bear witness

I am the testimony of a being
Searching in his emptiness
To find the opposite of my life
And call that holiness

With my faith
I created two homes

One of my dreams and hopes
One of my desire and fears
One full of life and visions
One full of desperate tears

In my faith
There is everything
Except a heaven
For heaven is a place of the mind
A place beyond life
A fantasy
Too good to believe
Too good to leave
A poison of thoughts
Of joy through greed
A false judgment of deeds

No, heaven is not a place of the earth
For those who try to create a heaven
Create often a thousand hells
And while they tell of prosperity
Thousands cry their tales

My faith tells me not to feed of hunger
Not to thrive through suffering
But see beyond the tears of innocence
And give love as an offering
My faith deprives the self from selfishness
And saves the self from madness

In my faith
There is a son
Free of hate
Filled only with love
Compassionate
He fills darkness with light
For the souls to see and learn
Of everything
And then to be

Of everything
He prays for the hateful
He prays for the predators
He prays for the pray
He says the truth gives freedom
He is the truth, the life, and the way
Then, the son becomes the father

In my faith
There is a mother
With a virgin soul
Untouched by the ways of the earth
Unharmed by harmful ways
A mother that I call when in fear
The possibility in my wishes
Unconditional and clear
A resting place for the wild
A safe embrace for the child

In my faith
There are sisters and brothers
That chose to not choose of selfish wealth
Giving their lives to my faith
To my comfort and health

My faith is my developing thoughts
Rage and tranquility
Beyond my understanding
That I long to learn
Of my surrealistic reality
My faith is my addiction
For believing and disbelieving
My will to see myself among everything
And feel what I'm achieving
To feel what I don't understand
To deny what I know
To see beyond my sight
Where time flows

My faith has no name
My faith has a way
My faith is not about God
Not about divinity
It's about a man
With faith in humanity
Lost in the consciousness of life
In love with itself
Unconscious in his feelings
To believe himself
My faith is not beyond the living
But the sole experience of life
And all the thoughts that can
Keep life living
And keeps dead moments alive
To grant a mortal being
The feeling of eternity
And a dying creature
A sense of dignity

My faith is simplicity
In a complex existence
And forever changing thoughts
With doubts of resistance

Creating a sacred song
That I can hear
That I can sing
A sanctified melody
Memorized by the mind
Turning winter to spring

My faith is not an answer
It is not a question
It is my being
My every moment
My ways
My self
My surroundings

The essence of my mind
My consciousness
Begins and ends
With my faith

The ways of love

Love can come as a blessing
Love can come as a curse
Growing within
Stretching outside
Changing your thoughts
With your own thoughts

Love is a state of life
In your mind
Conquering your vision
Capturing your senses
Freeing you from the impossible

If you love for honor
Love will someday bring disgrace
If for the sake of pleasure
No pleasure can come without pain
When you love for no reason
Love is the gain
Love is only love
For no reason
Love life
And life will give you
The possibility to love again

Love is not complicated
It is not exclusive
It grows more in the simplest of hearts
Love will melt you down
Into its mold
Shaped by illusions
And your submission
To an unknown fate
Love replaces faith
And makes you dream
To end your dream

And dedicate your everything
To love

Love is beyond human understanding
Fitting in the heart of everyone
Love is not about knowing
Rather about the unknown
Love is hunger
Not the nourishment
Wisdom at peace with foolishness
The creator of joy and beauty
An experience of wishful feelings
Laughter and cry
The unconditional surrender
To the force of life

Love dies when imprisoned
Among reasons
Love dies when chained
To a single entity
Love can only be born
And spread into eternity
Love is in every core
And your spirit
Opens or locks the door
For your love to be
In the heart of light
Consumed by life

The Mirrors of Truths and Lies

In my mind there is a story
In living thoughts
In solitude
In my mind there is a voice
never silent
yet subdued
In my mind there is a melody
and a beat
of rage and harmony
In me there is a song
of my truth
of joy and acerbity
In my mind there is a light
shining upon my thoughts
granting me sight
In my mind there are shadows
sharp edges
and poisonous arrows
In my mind there are roads
for me to walk
to carry heavy loads
In my mind there are mirrors
of truth and lies
and errors
and I live in unchosen races
on whatever path
to ever changing places
facing the mirrors of truths
facing the mirrors of lies
the mirror of myself
with multiple faces
some lost and empty
some full of faith
searching for traces
looking for the truths and lies
finding only reflections

and I memorize
an existence in motions
to fill my life with feelings
to fill my life with purpose
and to feel my addictions

My existence is surrealistic
My faith is my existence
My being grew in my body
My end a matter of distance
As the story finds a melody to become my song
and the light and shadows shapes my tranquility
I will walk on my road with my heavy load
and believe that my present is eternity

Lifeless in the heart of life

When you lose your faith in faith
And your choice is not your choice
When your words are not your words
And your voice is not a voice
When you forget what you should remember
And remember what you should forget
When your wishes are to not wish
And your hope is to regret

Lifeless in the heart of your life
Dreamless in a world of dreams
Heartless as your heart drowns
In the depth of many streams
You lose your faith in faith
And sorrow is your breath
And your wishes are to not wish
In a time of living death

Chapter 3 – Of Existence

In my world I exist with infinite images inside my mind
Human before humanity evolving with my thoughts
And the universe is me feeling my existence

Behind the name

They call me by name
And I answer
They call my name
And I invite them
to the thoughts
behind the name

Behind the name
Where I am my thoughts
and deeds
and mistakes
and needs

Behind the name
Where I am a story
Buried in my past
In my memories
In my frozen cast

Behind the mist
Stands a child
An unknown face
In an uncertain place

A child turning to a youth
Drunk with illusions
Seeking answers
To survive a mystery

Lessons learned
With a lost fantasy
With a broken heart
With unfounded harmony

Life became love
And deep wounds

Cut by sharp edges
of a lost history

Love became a song
A sad voice
Suffocated by emotions
Echoing my mentality
Behind the name
There is a human
Calm in solitude
An inseparable entity

Poor with wealth
Rich in poverty
Sane beyond madness
Mad beyond sanity

Behind the pride
Behind the shame
Inside my thoughts
Behind the name

The homeless woman

I ignore you
For I see you
And know that I am a part of your pain
Through you I see
The hidden reasons of my successes
And the success of my hideout

You are one of the children I have slaughtered
And laughter I have drained in sadness
To gain my comfort
To brighten my vision of life
For the sake of the lies I call my truth
Where I am human
By murdering humanity
Where I am more human than you

I see you
Yet I close my eyes
To blind my conscience
And numb my ethics
I ignore you
Coexisting
As if I choose
Not to exist

In my silent courage
I hear you scream
My crippled empathy
Walks through a dream
Where I cry your tears
And hate your fears
Where I reach the depth
To confront your killer
And my own face appears

Then I ignore you

For I see you
And wish not to taste your agony

Would you ignore me?
Do you ignore me?
Do you ignore my truth?
Tell me
If I offer you my helping hand
Will you accept?
And forget
Or read my poem
To unwrite the written

Do you ignore me?
Do you ignore my truth?
I wish you could take my smile once
And give sweetness a truthful name
I wish to have your tears once
To feel my guilt and shame

I ignore you
For I am the genius behind your misery
And the winner of your losses
I am the crucifier of good
A lie growing through history

A trash can in Prague

Five feet of distance
We are sharing time
Both of us are criminals
In an unknown crime

In a can I throw my waste
Leftovers of my greed
Only to see you, fellow man
Feed your need

Five feet away
Yet in a different world
Our painful thoughts hidden
In words unheard

Why am I frozen
Unable to enable my will
Why is your pride unmoved
Painfully standing still

What is the matter
My fellow man
Why is the plan of your life
Outside my plan

What do you look for
Inside the trash can
Is it my empathy
Or what used to make me human

Are you searching
For dignity
Outside my humanity
By not doing what I can

They tell me you are weak

They tell me you are sick
They tell me you lie
A thief doing his trick

Others say you are
The shadow of my well-being
The cramps of my joy
The senseless of my sense
The equal I destroy

But what I see
Is a being I never wish to be
A man lost in his life
I see you
Five feet away
From all my thoughts

Five feet away
From my joy
From the man you annoy

Away from all
Laws of words
Free in the prison
Of my justice
Where I am the criminal
And you serve my sentence
Five feet away from me
And I am five feet
Away from you
We are sharing time

A poor man's poem

I lost
Before competing
Stopped
Before starting
I woke up
In a world without mercy
In a place
Where my value is unseen
In a time
With moments lacking space
I am condemned
To dream the dreams of the unmerciful
I'm doomed
To mourn without tears

Sometimes
I see myself as you
Lacking my torment
Sometimes
I live your life
In a confusing moment
In my imagination
I live like you
Without becoming you
I have your sight
Without possessing your heart
I become you
Without leaving myself

I am blamed
For your doings
Judged by your measures
Punished by your norms
Sentenced to live
Imprisoned in shadows
Of your castles

Of lights
Then I am blamed
For living in the shadows

I am poor
Yet I can rhyme
All my feelings
With all the pain
And I survive
Knowing death
While I'm alive

Behind Sadness

There is a tear on your cheek
A sad song in your silence
Filling the depth of your emptiness
Where you seek
The secrets of the bottomless surface
Forming the logics of your madness
Where time is spent
Dreaming of the end
Until the broken
Is impossible to mend
Making you kneel
And kill your pride
As future changes
To present
To hide
In history
Torturing your mind

The Sound of the Duduk

The sound of the duduk brings the heavens and the mountains together

Where nature embraces the human soul bringing time to an endless end and life to an eternal thought

With closed eyes you will join the past in a moment of sadness created at your separation from the past

Sadness in the shape of beauty turning your vision to the voice of your mind singing the submission of all your feelings to love

From there you will mention limits only to explain the unlimited and speak not to be heard but to listen

Free to choose without knowing what to choose you will find your way

You will imagine your wishes, wished for you by your friends and your enemies

Then you will wish that you never wished

To the sound of the duduk your hopes melt in a prayer bringing the unborn to life in the sanctity of your pure heart

Then sweetness will touch the bitter part of your mind and you will repeat your prayer again

Oh, how sweet is the sound of the duduk

The sound of the lute

Does the sound of the lute make you sad
Or the muted tones that no other than you can hear
Break your harmony and shed your tears?
What are the secrets of your silence?
What is the hidden memory that you can't forget?
Speak for the world to know
Speak the truth
Speak sadness
Speak the shame
Of the dream that vanished
and love victimized by the civilized
Hear the waves of a world you knew
Hear the truth
Hear sadness
Feel shame
In laughing faces
Drowned in the blood of their innocence

What string of the lute plays your tune?
Is it the one with the muted sound
Heard only by your sorrow?

Close your eyes and pray
To have the wealth of the poor
The unexplained joy in a guiltless smile

And hum an old refrain
A melody that remains
Of the lost dream of pain
In a distant yesterday
And sing while astray
If people ask me about you
What will I answer?
What can I say?

Drink

Hoist your glass to welcome the saddest of thoughts
And drink with the traces of your loss
Dedicate your time to what you detest
Poison your sanity with the fluids of madness
To find harmony in your distress

Drink to drown the pain in your heart
Drink
Don't keep your soul and your eyes apart
Sing out your sorrow in the land of unconsciousness
Drink to deny the cause of sadness

Silent

Silent, though the atrocities of your surroundings
Silent, though the gift of speech

Painfully you protect the secrets of your existence
Deep, too deep for anyone to reach

You wish not to share your laughter
To avoid to share your cry

Far from the laws of human nature
Living your truth sheltered by a lie

Hiding inside orbits of thoughts
Captive in the webs of your memory

Your doings have become your tools of judgment
Justifying your present and your history

Silent to listen
Silent to hear
Silent to hide
To disappear

The ruins of my life

Among the ruins of my life
Among broken visions
Wrecks of great thoughts

In a fading truth
Alive in memories
Along the dying spirit of my youth
I find moments that I wish to relive

And moments I wish to forget
Haunting feelings frozen
Once a wish, now a regret

Wisdom turned to foolishness

And the precious decayed to waste
Sweetness turned bitter
In flavors lacking taste

There in the ruins, I once grew

And learned by my emotions
Imprisoned in doorless rooms
In castles of betrayals and devotions

Now my infinity is given an end

As lightness grows denser
Still confusion will not descend
For my question lacks an answer

Pure soul of a sinner

I see you
Orphaned by living parents
Banished from a rightful home
I see your happiness written briefly
On thin papers flying in a storm

I see you
In your eyes
Behind the surface of pain
Deep under your tears
Before you were abandoned
Before the birth of your fears
Before the violence
Tortured by the tortured
In their manifestation of goodness

Before they robbed your flesh
And humiliated your motherhood
Separating mother from daughter
Forcing you to be a sinner
In the eyes of their good
Mercifully committing the slaughter

Christians crucifying Christ
A thousand times
By judging the unjudgeable
With ignorance
Murdering their souls
When breaking the unbreakable

I see you
Stronger than evil
Bigger than your wounds
Higher than your fall

I see you

Struggling with your age
Playing with your childhood
Growing to be small

I see you
Believing in your future
While losing faith
Following an unknown guide

I see you
Crying in shame
Swallowing your truth
Defending your pride

I see you
Fighting furiously
Not wishing to fight

I see you
Existing in darkness
While embracing your light

The Owner

In my world
I am the center
I am the light
And when I close my eyes
Everything is darkened except my thoughts

In my world
I am perfect without errors
Gentle in my most inhuman views
With just a touch of imagination
I can brighten anything and everything

In my world I am visible
With no need to hide
No lies can change my shape
No smile can erase my scars

In my world I own everything I see
Everything I dream
All the feelings of life
In my world I am the owner

Pride

There is a world beneath my feet
There is a sky beyond my reach

Functionality in what I detest
Impossibility in what I preach

Still I insist to follow my path
Ready to sacrifice the most

Kneeling for nothing and no one but
The Father, the Son, and the Holy Ghost

There are senses in my essence
Living history in my presence

Filling my feelings with pride
To withstand my existence

In the world beneath my feet
Or in the sky beyond my reach

Dream, foolish man

Dream, foolish man
Of what you wish to be
And scream
Spread the waves of your agony
And curse in your cry
What you don't wish to fight
That you choose to call your destiny
Dream of anything
Except of being chosen
By the chosen
For the mystery of choice
Is the root of all mysteries

Art

Art is a word...unspoken
Until life finds a way to say it
Until lips move
And the air willingly carries it from sense to sense
Where art becomes a word of the soul

Art is a light...invisible
Until it reflects in a way that one's eye sees it
So it may shine the shady parts of one's awareness
Revealing all things

Art is a form....unshaped
Until formed by the ways of one's mind
And sensed when touching the spirit

Art is a game...yet played
Enlightening the child in you that seeks
Creating logic in your illogical mysteries

Art is a temple....unvisited
Until the core of faith
Kneels to pray for the unknown
Sanctifying the temple with belief

Art is a book...unprinted
Until knowledge reads its chapters
Liberating your intellect from its pages

The mountain of waste

Live of my waste
The bit of my wealth I grant you
Climb the hills of my waste
See, the might of my creation
See, I built a mountain for you to climb
Higher than the conscience of man
Bigger than the survival of humanity
See, how I paint the future
Darker than the past
Where even light is lethal
See me mastering death
By mistreating life

Unwise wisdom
Unsee what you see
See, the wealth I created
The mountains
The rivers
See life sacrificed for man
As if man was outside
The might of life

Live by the mountain
That I built to overcome my fear
Live of my mishaps
Live on the mountain of my perversity
Live by my pity and greatness
Live of my mistakes

See, I built a mountain for you to climb
Illustrating my madness and perversity
Higher than the conscience of man
Mightier than the survival of humanity

The rejected boy

I came from another land
Where my life lacks value
From another world
Where dreams are sins
I came from a world
Where death starts from within

I came to be with you
Do you wonder why?
Ask yourself
Why do I wish to be you?
Ask yourself
Why do I wish my truth to die?
Why you
If not to find what you found?
Why here
If not to experience
The things you love?

I am rejected
By you
For loving what you do
For dreaming your dreams
For asking
For thinking that I am your equal
For seeing myself with you
And you seeing me
With you

What excuse do I need
To live?
What value do I need
From you?
Who made you evaluate?
Who made you
If not you?

I am myself too
My rejected self
With all my will
All my faith
All fantasies and dreams
I am rejected

Now I am away from you
My days are away
My ways are away
My face is changed by time
My story is frozen
In metal
In your world of metals
My face is frozen
I am a sad moment
Born and died in time
A tear
Dried
And stained the memories
Of the ones that rejected
The poor boy

Now I will go to another land
Where my life lacks value
To another world
Where my dreams are sins
To a cursed world
To start dying from within

Fado

What is that sound
From a burning heart
Of a frozen soul
Singing Fado
Tales of struggling thoughts
In a peaceful mind
And eyes longing
To drown in pain
Illustrated in anger
In a lovely face
And wisdom begging
To be insane

What is that song
That reshapes my shape
What is wrong
When surreal words
In suffering sentences
Settle in your head
Like a poem of a dream
Of something unsaid

What is that torment
That makes you sing
As if your world
Is full of nothing
Reaching for everything
Out of your reach
In the echo of a rhyme
To the sound of strings
Following your line
Telling your story
Adding to my memories
Rekindling my history
With a fire of emotion
Encircling my existence

In a sweet bitter notion

Sing your Fado
Stretch the tones
And reform the melody
From solid to fluid
Then baptize my spirit
And feed my presence
With flavors of innocence
So I can taste the meaning
Of your Fado

Aunt Victoria

My dearest of memories
My first bit of essence
You who gave me without knowing
Without a thought
You who bought me everything you could
To build inside me what can't be bought

Gifts made of love
Tales made of gentle words
A teddy made of friendship
A sky filled with happy birds
Books full of wise fantasies
To write the path of my story

Somehow on that road
I left you
And I grew old
So did you
Hardships became your world
And I failed you

I seek my courage
So I could save you
From your fears
From my fear
In a guilty face

Baptized in tears
Wishing more
Doing less
Finding peace
In a sad mess
Love of a boy
In the shame of a man
Misery and joy
Of a broken pride

Longing to repay
Unable to provide

Prepared for success
I learned to fail
One of two minds
Two ways on one trail
My truth is survival
My lie is my truth
Of a forgotten child
Denied by a youth

In my dreams
I comfort you
In your distress
I deny you
I remember
Yet I forget you

My nostalgic smiles
My half-forgotten deeds
My pride in defeat
My unforgettable creeds

Many times I have wondered
What I would do if I could
And just as many times I've cried
That I have not done what I should

I imagine visiting
Your everyday life
I imagine you greeting me
I imagine you smiling
In tranquility
Losing your fear

But beyond imagining
I feel less
Like a pitiful man with grief

Hiding inside a shell
A miserable survivor
With a story to tell
Of the blend of feelings
Of sadness and pride
In a life not of choice
Choosing a side

I walked in my dream

I walked in my dream
On a road
Going down the hills of consciousness
Looking down
To see the place I will face
Looking up
To see the place I replaced
Forced to walk
Wishing to stop
But I was a part of the route and time
Sharing a dream with the elements of dreams
On my path of life
On the shore to nonliving
On one stream of two streams
Outlining the way of my ways
Clarifying the shape of my days
Knowing the end before the end

As I looked to the past
I saw a vision of humanity
I saw a warrior
A slayer of thousands
Injured by his sword
Poisoned by his courage
Enslaved by his faith
Betrayed by his loyalty

I saw a warrior
His eyes spoke of his emptiness
His body spoke of his fear
His hands tried to conceal all their works
He was separated from humanity
As humanity did not invite him
Into its comfort
But left him
Sacrificed him

To be the edge to inhumanity
To be the shield between
The soft core of humans
And the hard shell of life
A free man inside the prison of lies

Suddenly, death and birth appeared as twins
The facial lines of the worrier changed
To the lines of kings
Adorned with surreal wings
With the wisdom of a thief
Obsessed with owning things
Chained with golden rings
To be more than human
To be larger than the truth
Unlimited and endless
Blind and senseless
Sacrificing the living for the nonliving
Feeding on the innocence
To learn of the irrelevant

The past melted with a wind
Shaping a throne in a shadow
Of the king now unkinged
And his queen turned into a widow
I turned to follow the gravity of life
And to fear the memories of fear
Visions in darkness
In silence hearing what I wish not to hear
I still walked in my dream
Conscious in unconsciousness
In time running out
While the story was told
As I longed for youth
I grew old
In a frozen faith lie my wishes
In burning thoughts wondering why
As if life is a wish to wonder
From dead I arose, from life to die

My dream turns to torture
My sleep turns to cry
Living my truth
Dying to know why

82

I woke up from the dream

Then I woke up from the dream
Where I unconsciously thought my thoughts
Where I wondered, without wondering
Of the wise and the naughts
Where I unknowingly knew
Of everything I saw
And imagined that I was touched
By the law of no law

Now I'm awake
Now I'm enclosed in numbers
That man calls time
Yes, man who gave everything a name
Names to all that he fears
Names to everything he despises
All he oppresses and demeans
Naming life itself outside itself
Making me live in a wonder
Of whys and whos
A slave living under
The musts and the taboos

Now I'm awake
Yet I still start to dream
As sadness captures my free will
I look to follow the mainstream
But their numbers are standing still
Alone in a full space
Stranger in my place of birth
With many feelings to trace
And a meaning to unearth
Now I'm awake
Yet I still dream

A Student

I am life and the witness
Of the ways of my days
I am life inside
A thousand thousand lives
The silence and the words of a phrase
From nothing I came
To nothing I will return
A student of an ever-changing truth
Never understanding
What lessons to learn

About Life

What is pride
In a slave's mind
And what is a free man's
Way to hide
Inside the outside

How does man survive
When sentenced to death
Breathe the last moment
Or hold his breath

Is the meaning
Devoid of meaning
Is truth merely a sensation
Is a feeling
My reaction
To your reflection

Tell me, you who live
What is life
Tell me of living
Of aching
Of aging
Tell me of dying

Tell me
What is pride
In your mind
And where do you hide
Your freedom
Tell me
Will you breathe
Or hold your breath
When facing death

Beautiful Woman in a Cage

A woman sits in an open cage
Her life written on an empty page
Wondering if her calm or her rage
Will save her from her age

She hums a sad melody
To feel herself empathy
And dwell in her dead history
To hate her living reality

Sometimes she laughs and cries
Sometimes she hides and spies
On the mirror image of her lies
Fearing the unreachable skies

So she sits in her open cage
In her palm a key to her outrage
Planning what role to arrange
To show on an invisible stage

Hurt

Hiding
Inside a scar
Living with secrets of pain
Unable to undo what's done
Etched in the brain

Frozen
In a state of fear
Telling a story
Encased in tears

Hurt
Echoing within
With an unchanging beat
Ending only to begin

An angel robbed of her paradise
The known captured by the unknown
Fear silenced by crimes
While rage showing the unshown

Evil repeating its horrible ways
In the past of an innocent child
Torturing the body
By poisoning the mind

Hurt
With an unchanging beat
Echoing within
Ending only to begin

Refugee

I am a refugee
A deserter of his home
Running to nowhere
To where I may grieve
From the work of killers
In a world of thieves

I am a simple man
With a complicated fate
Born of love
Tormented by hate
Struck by the undesirable
With weightless weight

What protected me
Is now a wreckage
What gave me comfort
Is now a burned-out village
Fear has turned to despair
My empty gaze is my message

My roots are destroyed
My smile I bury
Beneath the sadness of my heart
Where I worry
And a mind filled with death
Like a crowded cemetery

The horrors of my days
Don't rest in my nights
They stay
And I try to pretend
And strive to survive
And stay

In the sorrowful melody

Humming within me
I find a tone of joy
I hear the laughter
Of a poor child
When I use to be a boy

Sometimes I try
To put a brief smile
On a worried face
But as memories return
And joy abandons me
My smile soon fades

I wander
And wonder
Where am I going?
Who am I forsaking
If not myself?
What am I doing?

Where will I find peace?
Every night my dream
Is not to dream
Every day my reality
Is a nightmare
Torture and screams

Will I ever love myself
and find rest?
In a home outside my home
Where will I find and build my nest?
Will I find and lose myself again?
Will I end in the east or west?

I don't want to lose
I don't want to win
I want to be in peace
I want to be myself
I have no idols

I have no greedy dreams
My wish is life
Simple and wonderful
Undisturbed life
I want to love
I want my family
No ideology
No theology
Only a life

What gave me comfort
Is now my grief
What sheltered me
Is now in ruins
My memories are full of sadness
As I embrace my concerns
To find a meaning in this madness

Every step away from my past
Every breath seems to be the last
Every experience of me
All living moments
Now frozen in my memory

As a song with a single tone
With a verse of irrelevant moan
And a loving heart
Now solidified to stone
Torturing my inside
The only side in my possession
With survival as obsession
Dying showing omission
And forced into deception

Look at me
You who can see me
See and judge me
You are not me
Please don't fear me

Please don't pity me
Help me

I wish not to kill
I wish not to die
Please don't make me beg more
Don't ask who and why
Just let me live
Let me be me
A helpless refugee

Rich man begging the beggar

I beg you
Not to beg me
I beg you
Hide the face
That I wish not to face
As you open your hand to receive
I close my ungiving heart
I beg you not to think
In my thoughts
Just find an answer
That eases my life
Not your distress
Why aren't you embarrassed
By what shames me
You speak what I can't hear
You live what I can't bear
What made you beg
Made me detest your begging
What made me beg
Made you detest your truth
I beg you
Not to beg me
I beg you
Hide the face
That I wish not to face